# CORPSE FLOWERS

# SMELL NASTY!

BY TAYLER COLE

Gareth Stevens
PUBLISHING

Please visit our website, www.garethstevens.com. For a free color catalog of all our high-quality books, call toll free 1-800-542-2595 or fax 1-877-542-2596.

Library of Congress Cataloging-in-Publication Data

Names: Cole, Tayler, author.
Title: Corpse flowers smell nasty! / Tayler Cole.
Description: New York : Gareth Stevens Publishing, [2017] | Series: World's weirdest plants | Includes bibliographical references and index.
Identifiers: LCCN 2016037132| ISBN 9781482456073 (pbk. book) | ISBN 9781482456080 (6 pack) | ISBN 9781482456103 (library bound book)
Subjects: LCSH: Amorphophallus–Juvenile literature. | Pollination by insects–Juvenile literature. | Plants–Adaptation–Juvenile literature.
Classification: LCC QK495.A685 C65 2017 | DDC 584/.64–dc23
LC record available at https://lccn.loc.gov/2016037132

First Edition

Published in 2017 by
**Gareth Stevens Publishing**
111 East 14th Street, Suite 349
New York, NY 10003

Copyright © 2017 Gareth Stevens Publishing

Designer: Katelyn E. Reynolds
Editor: Kristen Nelson

Photo credits: Cover, p. 1 DEA/C.DANI/De Agostini/Getty Images; cover, pp. 1–24 (background) Conny Sjostrom/Shutterstock.com; cover, pp. 1–24 (sign elements) A Sk/Shutterstock.com; p. 5 Alex Wong/Getty Images; p. 7 Isabelle OHara/Shutterstock.com; p. 9 (main) ideeone/E+/Getty Images; p. 9 (inset) Georgialh/Wikipedia.com; p. 11 (main) CHRIS KLEPONIS/AFP/Getty Images; p. 11 (inset) Douglas Graham/CQ Roll Call Group/Getty Images; p. 13 Hardyplants at English Wikipedia/Wikipedia.org; p. 15 A J Withey/Moment Open/Getty Images; p. 17 Stuart C. Wilson/Getty Images; p. 19 PAUL J. RICHARDS/AFP/Getty Images; p. 20 Rich Carey/Shutterstock.com; p. 21 ZACH GIBSON/AFP/Getty Images.

All rights reserved. No part of this book may be reproduced in any form without permission in writing from the publisher, except by a reviewer.

Printed in China

CPSIA compliance information: Batch #CW17GS : For further information contact Gareth Stevens, New York, New York at 1-800-542-2595.

# CONTENTS

Words in the glossary appear in **bold** type the first time they are used in the text.

# ROTTEN FLOWER

Travel to **tropical** Indonesia, and you might come across an awful, rotting smell. It's not something dead, but the smell of the **corpse** flower. This flower is one of the largest in the world, able to grow to be 10 feet (3 m) tall! But that's not what makes this plant weird.

When it **blooms**, the corpse flower smells like rotting flesh! Scientists believe the smell is meant to draw in, or attract, bugs such as sweat bees, **carrion** beetles, and flesh flies.

## SEEDS OF KNOWLEDGE

The name "corpse flower" comes from the Indonesian words bunga bangkai. "Bunga" means "flower," and "bangkai" means "corpse" or "cadaver."

The smell of the corpse flower is said to be very strong even from far away.

# HOUSE OF ROT

The corpse flower is native to the rainforests of Sumatra, Indonesia. These tropical rainforests are located close to the **equator** and get a lot of rain all year. That's perfect for corpse flowers, which like wet soil when they're ready to bloom.

Corpse flowers are very picky about where they live. There must be high heat and high **humidity**. The corpse flower is likely to be found in clearings on hillsides throughout the rainforest where it can get enough light.

Many corpse flowers are grown in special indoor gardens called botanical gardens. They're often grown in rooms that mimic, or copy, the heat and humidity of their rainforest home.

Amorphophallus titanum
ARACEAE
Sumatra

# SMELLY STRUCTURE

The corpse flower starts as a seed. It grows small leaves and a **tuber** called a corm. Every time the plant grows a new leaf, the corm gets bigger, too. Most years, the plant *only* grows a huge leaf.

The first flower for a young plant can take 7 to 10 years to appear. Then, the plant appears to grow a flower around every 3 years. The flower has a tall, fat part in the middle called the spadix. A large, petallike part called the spathe surrounds the spadix. Inside the spathe, at the bottom of the spadix, are tiny flowers.

## SEEDS OF KNOWLEDGE
Altogether, the spadix, spathe, and tiny flowers are called an inflorescence.

The leaf of the corpse flower looks like a small tree and can grow up to 20 feet (6 m) high.

leaf

corm

# PUTRID PERFUME

The corpse flower only blooms for one night! When it's nearing the time to bloom, the plant can grow as much as 4 inches (10 cm) a day! Once the flower is ready, its **internal** temperature rises to 98°F (37°C).

While it heats up, the flower also begins to give off its terrible smell. The heat, smell, and deep red color of the spathe mimic a dead human body to attract bugs that eat or lay eggs in rotting meat.

## SEEDS OF KNOWLEDGE

The smell the corpse flower gives off has the same **chemicals** in it as stinky cheese, rotting fish, and sweaty socks. Ew!

When **botanists** say a corpse flower is blooming, that means the spathe has opened up. While this looks a lot like a flower, the plant's actual flowers can't really be seen inside the spathe when in bloom!

spadix

spathe

before bloom

# POLLINATION

The corpse flower is stinky for a good reason—to draw bugs in! But why does it need the bugs? Like other plants, this odd plant's tiny flowers need to be pollinated in order for it to reproduce.

The thousands of tiny flowers inside the spathe are split into two groups. Half are female flowers, and half are male. When the spathe opens, the female flowers are ready for pollination! As the spathe begins to **wilt**, so do the female flowers.

## SEEDS OF KNOWLEDGE

Pollination is part of the **fertilization** of a flowering plant. Pollen must be moved from one flower to another, often on the legs and bodies of bugs.

12

The female and male flowers aren't open at the same time so the plant can't pollinate itself. That could lessen future plants' chance of survival.

flowers

15

# FRUITFUL FLOWER

The corpse flower commonly stays open for only about 12 hours. It begins blooming midafternoon, the smell increases throughout the night, and then both may be gone by morning! However, the bugs it draws in can be trapped inside the spathe for almost a day. They can't climb the smooth walls of the spathe.

Once pollinated, the flowers grow a big **stalk** of small red-orange berries. The berries have seeds inside them. They're eaten by animals and spread throughout the rainforest in their waste.

After the fruit is fully grown, the spathe falls off, leaving the fruit to be seen by nearby animals.

# STINKY DISCOVERY

In 1878, Italian botanist Odoardo Beccari was the first scientist to write about the corpse flower, which he saw in Indonesia. After Beccari's account, the plant's seeds were brought back to Kew Gardens in London, England, where people saw—and smelled—the first bloom in 1889.

Since then, the corpse flower has been grown in botanical gardens throughout the world. That means every year it's likely there's somewhere in the world where visitors can see—and smell—a corpse flower blooming!

On April 22, 2016, this corpse flower bloomed at Kew Gardens in London.

# FAMOUS FLOWERS

Because the corpse flower's bloom doesn't happen often, each flower's appearance is an exciting event, especially for botanists who have taken care of a nonblooming corpse flower for many years. Often, botanical gardens film the weird plant's growth and invite people from the community to witness it.

The tallest corpse flower bloom grew in 2010 in New Hampshire. It measured 10 feet 2.25 inches (3.1 m) tall! The largest corm weighed in at 258 pounds (117 kg) in Germany in 2006.

## SEEDS OF KNOWLEDGE

Each year after the leaf dies, the corm needs to be replanted. Older corms commonly weigh between 55 and 110 pounds (25 and 50 kg).

As interest in corpse flowers increases, more and more plants are grown throughout the world. It's not uncommon for there to be five or more blooms worldwide each year!

# DISAPPEARING CORPSE?

The rainforest home of the corpse flower is being cut down in order to clear land for palm plantations, or large farms, in Sumatra. Indonesia has lost more than 70 percent of its rainforest to human activity like this! Clearing the forest also harms the rhinoceros hornbill. This bird eats the fruit of the corpse flower and spreads its seeds.

Luckily, many people find this smelly plant captivating and continue to grow and study it. We don't want to lose this weird plant!

deforestation

# LIFE CYCLE OF THE CORPSE FLOWER

## Flower cycle
This can happen every 3 years after the first bloom, which takes 7 to 10 years.

The corm starts leaf and flower cycles.

## Leaf cycle
This happens most years. The leaf looks like a tree, and dies every 12 to 18 months.

spadix

spathe

A bud emerges.

The spathe and spadix develop.

The spathe opens.

The spadix wilts.

The spadix falls off. The spathe dies.

The fruit grows.

leaflets

leaf

corm

Courtesy of the Chicago Botanic Garden

# GLOSSARY

**bloom:** to be in flower. Also, the flower itself.

**botanist:** someone who is an expert in the science of plants

**carrion:** a dead, rotting animal

**chemical:** matter that can be mixed with other matter to cause changes

**corpse:** a dead body

**equator:** an imaginary line around Earth that is the same distance from the North and South Poles

**fertilization:** the adding of male cells to female cells

**humidity:** moisture in the air

**internal:** inside or the inner part of something

**stalk:** a plant part much like a stem

**tropical:** having to do with the hot parts of Earth near the equator

**tuber:** a short, thick, fleshy stem that forms underground and stores energy and from which a new plant can grow

**wilt:** to become floppy

# FOR MORE INFORMATION

## Books

Artell, Mike. *Pee-yew! The Stinkiest, Smellist Animals, Insects and Plants on Earth!* Tucson, AZ: Good Year Books, 2007.

Ganeri, Anita. *Peculiar Plants.* Chicago, IL: Raintree, 2013.

## Websites

**The Nonfiction Minute: Morty Makes a Stink**
*nonfictionminute.com/the-nonfiction-minute/morty-makes-a-stink*
Listen to a visitor's experience as she sees Morty the corpse flower.

**Rainforest Alliance: Forest Facts**
*rainforest-alliance.org/kids/facts*
Find out more about where the corpse flower lives!

**Publisher's note to educators and parents:** Our editors have carefully reviewed these websites to ensure that they are suitable for students. Many websites change frequently, however, and we cannot guarantee that a site's future contents will continue to meet our high standards of quality and educational value. Be advised that students should be closely supervised whenever they access the Internet.

# INDEX